## Titles from Finding My Way Books

*I Want To Be Like Poppin' Joe*
*Kaitlyn Wants To See Ducks*
*I Don't Know If I Want a Puppy*
*Marco and I Want To Play Ball*
*OE Wants It To Be Friday*
*Waylen Wants To Jam*

## Growing With Grace Series

*MyaGrace Wants To Make Music*
*MyaGrace Wants To Get Ready*

## Finding My World Series

*Neema Wants To Learn*
*Onika Wants To Help*
*Matteo Wants To See What's Next*
*Claire Wants a Boxing Name*

## Learning My Way Series

*Colors On My Papers/Rangi Za Makaratasi Yetu*
*Looking For Our Families/Kuangalia Familia Zetu*
*Fronts For Our Backs/Nyuso Kwa Migongo Yetu*
*Feelings at School/Les sentiments à l'école*
*Shapes at School/Les formes à l'école*
*My Amazing Body at School/Mon incroyable corps à l'école*
*Friends at School/Les amis à l'école*
*Places at School/Les endroits à l'école*
*Opposites at School/Les contraires à l'école*

Bilingual titles are also available

# Claire Wants a Boxing Name

A True Story Promoting Inclusion and Self-Determination

Finding My World Series

Jo Meserve Mach
Vera Lynne Stroup-Rentier

*Photography by Mary Birdsell*

TOPEKA, KANSAS

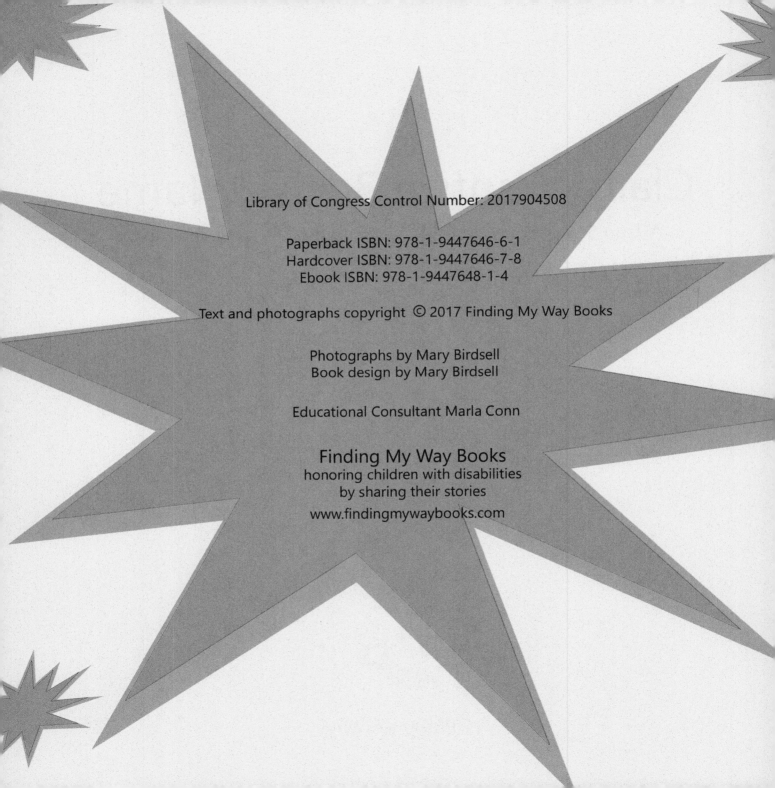

Library of Congress Control Number: 2017904508

Paperback ISBN: 978-1-9447646-6-1
Hardcover ISBN: 978-1-9447646-7-8
Ebook ISBN: 978-1-9447648-1-4

Photographs by Mary Birdsell
Book design by Mary Birdsell

Educational Consultant Marla Conn

**Finding My Way Books**
honoring children with disabilities
by sharing their stories
www.findingmywaybooks.com

Hi, my name is Claire.
I have lots of energy.

My mom and I are learning to box.
Boxing helps me use up my energy.

This is Vivian.
She's our boxing coach.

Vivian has different sight ability.
Her dog, Catcher, and I help her find the boxing club. Catcher's harness is on.
This means he is paying attention and working.

We found it.
The boxing club is huge!

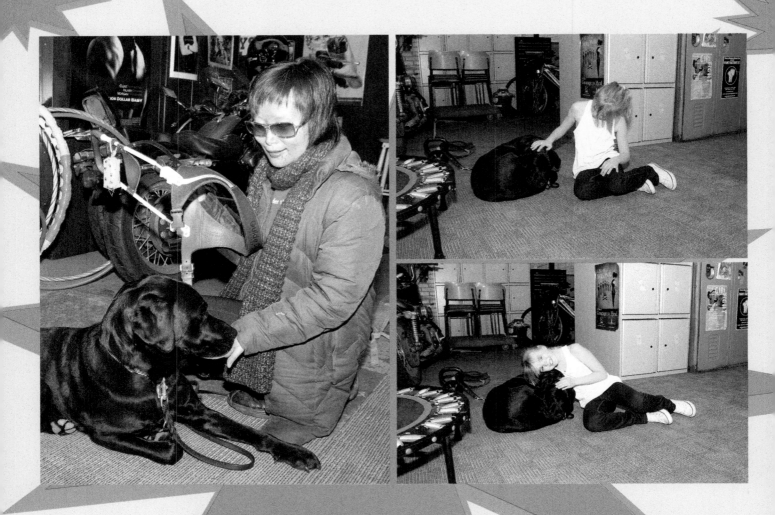

Catcher knows where to go.
Vivian takes off his harness.
He doesn't have to work here.
Now I can pet him.

I change my clothes for our boxing lesson.
I look at the lockers.
I like to see the boxers' names on them.

Today Vivian is going to tell me my boxing name.
It's an honor to get a boxing name.
You have to earn it.
Vivian's boxing name is Eraser.

Vivian talks to Savoy about my boxing name.
Savoy is the boxing club owner.
I wonder what my name will be.

I have to wait to learn my name.
It's time to warm up.
Savoy makes a chart for our practice.
It tells us what we need to do.

We get into the ring to start jumping rope.
Vivian wants us to jump fast.

Next we do push-ups.
Vivian says we need strong arms to box.

I take a break and rest with Catcher.
Mom and Vivian do even more push-ups.
I'd better go back!

Now it's hula hoop time.
Vivian is really good at this.
She keeps her attention on her movement.
I learn a lot by watching Vivian.

Vivian yells, "Cartwheel arms!"
She knows I love doing cartwheels.

I keep thinking about my boxing name.
I tell Mom I hope it isn't Claire Cartwheel.
I don't like that name.

Vivian says it's time to shadow box.
Shadow boxing makes me think of dancing.
I copy Vivian's actions as we move.

I count in my head. I step 1, 2, 3, 4.
We move forward and backward.
We move side to side.
I pay attention to how we move.

Then I punch, 5, 6.
Pow! POW!
The biggest punch is with my more powerful arm.

I need a cartwheel break.
I hope I get my boxing name soon.

Savoy teaches us a boxing move.
It's called the *Blender*.

21

I like the *Blender*.
I feel strong.

Vivian teaches me how to wrap my hands.
This will keep me from hurting them when I box.

Next we practice punching the bags.
This is the double-end bag.
It looks like a peanut.

I want to hit it like Vivian hits it.
She knows how to punch.

This is the speed bag.
Vivian is really good at hitting it.

Vivian can hit the same spot each time.
I have to pay attention.

Savoy has boxing gloves for me.
I wear them to box on the heavy bag.

Now I look like a real boxer.
Maybe I'll get a boxing name soon.
This bag is hard to hit.

I need a break with Catcher.
I want a boxing name that's awesome like Mom's.
Her boxing name is Slice n' Dice.

Vivian's ready to tell me my boxing name!
She says it's Laser Beam!
It's totally awesome!

I'm honored that Vivian gave me the name
Laser Beam.
I'm learning to focus my energy.
I hope I can become a boxer like Vivian!

*Thank you to Claire, her family, Vivian and Savoy for sharing their story.*

think outside the ring!

torontonewsgirls.com

We celebrate Claire's and Vivian's story!

Claire is ten years old and full of life! She loves singing, dancing, swimming, skating, and tumbling. Claire was born with a facial difference. Occasionally, she has to explain her looks to others, but she doesn't let this limit her in any way. She is very determined to live her life to the fullest.

Vivian describes herself as, "differently sight abled," and has a Seeing Eye dog, Catcher. She helped write Claire's story by contributing her perspective as a teacher and mentor. She wanted Claire to learn the value of paying attention because paying attention strengthens abilities.

Vivian spends a lot of time paying attention to what she is doing. It took her two years to understand her body sensations while she is boxing. She had to learn the placement of her hand and the timing of when to make contact with the bag. When she is shadow boxing, she pays attention to the distance between her feet and the sound of her movements. Vivian is always modifying her workout routine based on her changing sensations. This takes time and attention.

Catcher, Vivian's dog, also teaches Claire the importance of paying attention. When he is wearing his harness and working, he must stay attentive so Vivian can avoid obstacles as she walks. It is his job to protect Vivian and he works very hard. Vivian and Catcher are wonderful role models demonstrating self-determination.

We are empowered to share their story,
~Jo, Vera and Mary

33

# Vocabulary Glossary

Boxing - sport where you fight with your fists

Attention - focusing all your thoughts on what you're doing

Harness - straps that fit together on an animal

Owner - person that something belongs to

Push-up - a floor exercise where you use only your arms to move your whole body up and down

Cartwheel - action when someone moves like a wheel; throwing hands down to the ground one at a time with feet up and then pushing forward to land back on feet

## Information and Discussion Ideas for Educators

Self-determination is the ability to choose the life you want to live.

All children should be taught, at an early age, the skills needed for self-determination.

Without access to activities and the ability to participate in those same activities, children with disabilities are often limited in their opportunities to develop these skills.

Some of the skills needed are: choice making, self-awareness, problem solving, decision-making, self-direction, social connections and relationships, communication, responsibility, goal setting, and self-advocacy.

Here is an example of how the child in this story is learning one of these skills.
Story pages demonstrating self-regulation: 1, 2, 13, 20, 30

Discussion: Claire describes herself as someone who has a lot of energy. She knows that sometimes it's a challenge to pay attention. As she learns to box she needs to pay attention to Vivian's instructions while she builds her strength and practices boxing moves. If she has extra energy she does cartwheels. If she needs a break she spends time with Catcher. What are some of the things you do during the day to use up your energy? How do you take a break when you need one?

### For additional information visit www.findingmywaybooks.com.

**Finding My Way Books** bring together Jo Meserve Mach with her experience in Occupational Therapy, Dr. Vera Lynne Stroup-Rentier with her special education experience and continuing delight in raising two children with special needs, Mary Birdsell with her speech and theatre teaching experience and professional photography, and MyaGrace Rentier with her gift of enthusiasm. Together they follow their passion to promote inclusion and self-determination!

CPSIA information can be obtained
at www.ICGtesting.com
Printed in the USA
LVOW05s0331190218
567090LV00015B/42/P